Hope Without Borders

"This little book is incredible! I felt my heart come alive with every word. Mother Cabrini was tenacious, undeterred by insults and illness, and motivated by a deep love for Jesus. Every day of her life was an adventure in surrendering everything to God. At a time when millions of people are forced to flee their homeland as migrants and refugees, the world needs the inspiration of Mother Cabrini more than ever. May you be inspired to act with the same courage and joy in whatever your call—but especially in service to the most vulnerable among us."

Beth Knobbe
Author, speaker, and senior trainer for Catholic Relief Services

"As an immigrant and a former New Yorker, I have always felt a deep connection to St. Frances Xavier Cabrini because her story embodies the resilience and faith of those who leave everything behind to follow God's call.

Cattapan's heart for Mother Cabrini shines on every page, inviting us not just to admire this saint but to follow in her footsteps and say yes to God's plan—even when it sends us to the ends of the earth."

Mariana Pimiento
Founder of Big Apple Catholic

"As a Jesuit priest, I am struck by how Mother Cabrini was shaped by the Spiritual Exercises of St. Ignatius and how she embodied the missionary spirit of her namesake, St. Francis Xavier. Despite her fear of water, she repeatedly crossed the sea, bringing hope to countless people. This lovely devotional invites us to follow her example of finding God in all things and allowing Christ to be our captain. In a world desperately needing missionaries of hope, these thirty days with Mother Cabrini will inspire readers to make their own hearts a blank page for Christ to write upon."

Fr. Michael Rossmann, SJ
"One-Minute Jesuit" on Instagram
Author of *The Freedom of Missing Out*

Hope Without Borders

GREAT SPIRITUAL TEACHERS

30 DAYS WITH

Frances Xavier Cabrini

Edited by Amy J. Cattapan

Ave Maria Press AVE Notre Dame, Indiana

Quotations from Mother Cabrini's letters and retreat notes are taken with permission from the following:
Frances Xavier Cabrini, *Journal of a Trusting Heart: Retreat Notes of St. Frances Xavier Cabrini 1876–1911* (Claretian Publications, 2023).
Frances Xavier Cabrini, *Letters from the Voyages of St. Frances Cabrini* (Catholic Treehouse, 2024).

Series editor: John Kirvan

Founded in 1865, Ave Maria Press is a ministry of the United States Province of Holy Cross.

www.avemariapress.com

Paperback: ISBN-13 978-1-64680-403-0

E-book: ISBN-13 978-1-64680-404-7

Cover art © Matthew Watters.

Cover and text design by Katherine Robinson Coleman.

Printed and bound in the United States of America.

Contents

Timeline

1850	Francesca Cabrini is born on July 15 in Sant'Angelo di Lodi in the Lombardy region of Italy.
1857	Cabrini is confirmed on July 1.
1868	Cabrini receives her teacher's certificate at age eighteen.
1872–1874	Cabrini teaches at a public school in Vidardo, Italy.
1877	September 14: Cabrini takes religious vows and adds Saverio (the Italian form of Xavier) to her name in honor of her missionary hero, St. Francis Xavier.
1880	November 14: Mother Cabrini's order gets its start in Codogno with a Mass said by her friend Msgr. Serrati.
1880	December: The bishop of Lodi gives formal approval for Cabrini's order, originally titled the Missionary Salesians of the Sacred Heart.
1884	The Missionary Sisters open a house in Milan, Italy.

1887 September: Cabrini heads to Rome to get approval for the Rule of her order and to seek permission to open a house in Rome.

December 16: Archbishop Michael Augustine Corrigan of New York asks Bishop Scalabrini to send him "*good* Italian priests"[1] to help with the Italian immigrants of New York.

1888 March 12: The Rule for the order is approved by the Vatican.

December: Cabrini, having been urged by Bishop Scalabrini to head to America to help the Italian immigrants but wanting to go to China, returns to Rome to consult Pope Leo XIII.

1889 February 16: Cabrini writes to Archbishop Corrigan, informing him that she hopes to set sail for New York in May, if not sooner.

March 19: Mother Cabrini and six of her sisters leave Codogno, Italy, for the trip to America, making stops in

Milan, Paris, and Le Havre before crossing the Atlantic Ocean.

March 31: Cabrini and her six sisters arrive in New York City, much earlier than Corrigan expected them. He urges them to return to Italy since he has been unable to find an appropriate location and funding for them. Mother Cabrini refuses to leave, stating that she is there under obedience to the pope.

April 21: The sisters move into 43 East 49th Street in New York.

July 20: Cabrini heads back to Rome with two Irish girls as postulants.

1890 April 18: Cabrini returns to New York with seven sisters. Cabrini and her sisters move to Manresa (a former Jesuit residence), now named West Park.

1891 June 26: Archbishop Corrigan asks Cabrini to take over the administration of a hospital for Italians.

1891–1892	Cabrini spends time in Nicaragua to open missions there.
1892	April: On her way back from Nicaragua to New York, Cabrini stops in New Orleans, where Italians had been lynched the prior year. Seeing how demoralized the Italian immigrants were there, she promises to send back some sisters when she can.
	July: Cabrini sends three sisters from New York to New Orleans to prepare for the mission there.
	August 6: Mother Cabrini visits New Orleans again, bringing four more sisters with her.
1895–1896	Cabrini extends her missions into Panama and Argentina.
1899	Spring: Cabrini sends sisters to open a school in Chicago.
	October 10: The name of the order is officially changed to the Missionary Sisters of the Sacred Heart.

1902	Sisters from Argentina are sent to open a college in São Paulo, Brazil, and a school for the children of Italian immigrants is opened in Denver, Colorado.
1903	Cabrini's great friend, Pope Leo XIII, dies.
1904	Cabrini opens an orphanage in the northern part of Denver, Colorado, to care for the children orphaned by Italian immigrants working in the dangerous mines.
1905	April 26: Columbus Hospital is opened in Chicago.
1909	October 9: Cabrini becomes an American citizen.
1911	July 16: Columbus Extension Hospital is dedicated on the West Side of Chicago to expand the work of the original hospital.

1915	April 26: Cabrini purchases the Perry Hotel in Seattle, which later becomes a hospital.
1917	December 22: Mother Cabrini dies in Columbus Hospital in Chicago while working on Christmas gifts for children.
1928	The cause for Cabrini's beatification begins in Chicago.
1938	November 13: Cabrini is beatified by Pope Pius XI.
1946	July 7: Frances Xavier Cabrini is canonized by Pope Pius XII, making her the first American citizen saint.
1950	St. Frances Xavier Cabrini is named the Universal Patroness of Immigrants.

WHO IS

Frances Xavier Cabrini?

Francesca Cabrini was born two months premature on July 15, 1850, in the Lombardy province of Italy. She was so small and weak that her parents feared for her, and illnesses plagued this five-foot-tall saint her whole life. However, neither her lack of height nor her poor health kept her from traveling the world to bring the love of Jesus to all people.

At a young age, she decided she wanted to be a missionary like her hero, the great Jesuit priest St. Francis Xavier (from whom she later took her religious name). Like him, she also wanted to travel to the East as a missionary. Specifically, she hoped to head to China. As a child, she made paper boats, filled them with violets, and set them afloat down the river near her uncle's house, pretending that she was sending her missionaries to far-off lands. One day, she fell into the river as she played and nearly drowned. This near-death experience caused health issues and a fear of open water. Nevertheless, she still dreamed of becoming a missionary. As a young woman, she tried to enter two religious orders but was turned down due to her health issues.

Instead, she spent two years as a public elementary school teacher in Vidardo, where Frances won over the students with her gentle yet firm approach. She quickly became known for being humble yet dignified and for being a great organizer and leader despite her rather shy nature.

She caught the attention of her pastor, who asked her to take over an orphanage for girls in Codogno. This work eventually led her to form a community with seven of her girls. This community became the Missionary Sisters of the Sacred Heart of Jesus. At last, Frances believed she was beginning the missionary work she had always desired.

Inspired by her hero St. Francis Xavier, Mother Cabrini infused her new religious community with a spirituality similar to that of St. Ignatius of Loyola, founder of the Jesuits. Mother Cabrini made it a point for her and her sisters to reflect regularly on the life of Christ as detailed in St. Ignatius's Spiritual Exercises. Often, this came in the form of an annual retreat. However, she also encouraged her sisters to partake in a monthly retreat, as well as to take very short retreats at least once a week to examine how God was moving in their lives.

With her new community well underway in Codogno, Frances traveled to Rome to meet with the cardinal vicar, Msgr. Lucido Parocchi. She had two goals: to start a school in Rome and to get approval for the rule of her order so that they would become a pontifical institute. The cardinal, unsure of whether he should lend his support to yet another institute in Rome, told Frances to ask God for a sign by procuring five hundred thousand lire for the school.

Instead of being disheartened by his lack of enthusiasm, she displayed her characteristic total dependence on God and told the nun who was with her, "Courage, daughter! You will see that the Lord will change his heart."[2] Sure enough, the next time they met, the cardinal told her to open not one, but two schools: one free school for the poor in Porta Pia and another in the Sabine Hills where a kindergarten was needed.

After opening multiple schools in Italy, Frances was sure her next step would be to the East. However, when she met with Pope Leo XIII, he told her to head west. The archbishop of New York had asked for help with the plight of hundreds of thousands of Italian immigrants, most of whom were poor peasants. They struggled to find work, their children often played in the streets because they did not have access to proper schools, and their mortality rate was high since discrimination against Italians kept them from accessing quality hospitals. Furthermore, the lack of priests to preach in Italian meant they were losing touch with their faith, an integral part of their culture in the homeland.

Disappointed at first in the direction she and her missionary sisters were asked to travel, Frances and her sisters nonetheless accepted their assignment. When they arrived in New York, however, the archbishop tried to send them back. He had been unable to find the right facilities and funding for their mission. Undeterred, Frances refused to leave. She traveled to the Little Italy neighborhood of New York on foot to minister to the families living in the tenements and managed to establish an orphanage. Her success is all the more remarkable because wealthy New Yorkers often refused to contribute to her charitable work. She was slighted for various reasons: her Italian ancestry, her frail appearance, and her poor English skills.

For the next twenty-seven years of her life, Mother Cabrini traveled back and forth between North America, Europe, and Central and South America, establishing schools, orphanages, and hospitals. Although she had a fear of water, she used her Atlantic crossings as retreat times. Like the Jesuits,

Mother Cabrini believed in seeing God in all things. Through her letters and retreat journals, we see her repeatedly describe the splendor of God's creation as she sailed from continent to continent. From these times of prayer, her soul was fortified to face the challenges in her next destination. And just as the Jesuits believed in doing "all things for the greater glory of God," Mother Cabrini instructed her sisters to do "all for the greater glory of the Sacred Heart of Jesus."[3]

By the time she died in 1917, fifteen hundred women had joined the Missionary Sisters of the Sacred Heart of Jesus, with sixty-seven houses of sisters in eight different countries dedicated to education, nursing, and the care of orphans. Wherever they went, they continued to build the empire of hope that Cabrini had begun.

As you read through this thirty-day retreat with selections from Mother Cabrini's own retreat journals and letters, may you be inspired to be a missionary of hope, continuing Mother Cabrini's desire to bring the love of the Sacred Heart of Jesus to all people.

HOW TO
Use This Book

The books in the Great Spiritual Teachers series provide an introduction to the spiritual insights and wisdom of some of history's most extraordinary saints. Through these pages, you're invited to a place beyond mere reading, into an experience of daily prayer and meditation. You'll be accompanied by a spiritual teacher whose wisdom will awaken, enrich, and empower your walk with the Lord.

In other words, these books take you on a spiritual journey.

We have some suggestions for how you can make the most of this journey. But keep in mind that these books are meant to help you experience the freedom and joy of communing with God in prayer. The daily format is there to help—but don't hesitate to go at your own pace or take your own route! Repeat a day as often as you like, or skip a day if the reading isn't resonating with where you are in your journey. The goal is to hear the voice of God through the words of the saints.

However you choose to use this book, it's helpful to understand the thinking behind the format used for each day. We've chosen to follow the suggestion of the classic book on spirituality *The Cloud of Unknowing*, which describes a three-part movement of *reading, reflecting,* and *praying*: "These three are so linked together that there can be no profitable reflection without first reading or hearing. Nor will beginners or even the spiritually adept come to true prayer without first taking time to reflect on what they have heard or read."

Throughout these thirty days, you'll follow in the footsteps of this longstanding tradition. Each day starts with a section called "My Day Begins," in which you'll find a passage quoted or adapted from a great spiritual teacher. This is followed by "All Through the Day," which provides a short, memorable phrase (drawn from or based on the reading) that you can carry with you throughout the day, enabling you to reflect and meditate on a key truth, question, or insight. In the final section, "My Day Is Ending," you're encouraged to find a quiet place to go to the Lord in prayer, drawing on that day's reading as you lift up your petitions and praises to him.

My Day Begins

One of the best ways you can begin your day is to put yourself in the company of a great spiritual teacher.

The selected passages are short—just a few hundred words. But they are powerful! They've been chosen specifically for their ability to provide spiritual focus for your day and to remind you that you are a spiritual being, intended for relationship and intimacy with God.

These morning readings don't just put you in the presence of a spiritual teacher who can accompany you on your journey—they are also designed to invite you into God's presence so you can start your day in conversation with him.

If you find that you don't fully understand the reading, don't be discouraged! Understanding may come with time, meditation, and further prayer. For now, focus on your heart's response. Tell the Lord about the questions you have, and ask him for wisdom and insight.

It's also helpful to read *slowly*. We've divided the passages into sense lines to help you do just that. Instead of rushing through the reading, savor each word. Pay attention to which phrases or images resonate in your heart. Make room for God to speak. In short, read prayerfully. Each day's opening reading is meant to foster attentiveness to God and an attitude of readiness to hear what he wants to say to you.

All Through the Day

After the day's reading, you'll find a single sentence, a meditation that you can reflect on throughout your day. As you move forward with the busyness of everyday life, return to this reflection as often as you can. Try writing it down on a card and placing it somewhere you'll see it frequently. Or copy it down in a journal or planner. Recite it in the little free moments between tasks and conversations.

This reflection shouldn't take you out of the day's responsibilities. Rather, it should serve as a gentle reminder of God's presence within the many activities and tasks that make up your day—and an expression of your desire to live in connection with him.

My Day Is Ending

No matter what your day has brought to you, there's great wisdom in reaching the end of it and turning everything over to God in prayer, intentionally setting your mind and heart on him, and listening for his voice.

If you find that it's not easy to let go of the events of the day, to find peace and closure and solace in God's presence, here are some suggestions to help you:

1. Find a quiet, distraction-free place that you can return to each evening.
2. Quiet your spirit. Sometimes this involves relaxing your body and letting go of physical tension. Try adopting a posture that reminds you that you are in God's presence: sit or kneel; fold your hands or lift them up—whatever works for you. Focus on breathing deeply and deliberately.
3. When you feel calm and at peace, focus on the evening prayer phrase by phrase. If you find yourself getting caught up in analyzing the words of the prayer, wrestling with the meaning of a phrase, or becoming distracted, don't worry! Just pause, breathe, and begin again. Set aside all the distractions and worries that stand between you and God.

The time spent with the evening prayer doesn't need to be very long—just remember that it is a time of expressing complete trust and confidence in God, preparing yourself for a night of peaceful sleep. End the day as you began it, resting in his presence.

Some Other Ways to Use This Book

1. *Create your own reflections.* If the provided "All Through the Day" reflection doesn't resonate with you, or if you'd like to add to it, feel free to choose another phrase or image from the morning reading that caught your attention.
2. *Incorporate journaling into your spiritual journey.* Many find that journaling—either through copying out the provided reflections and prayers or writing your own—is an excellent way to slow down and focus, ensuring that your mind doesn't skip over important insights. Or, you could use a journal to keep a record of your experiences on this thirty-day journey, such as the insights that had the biggest impact on your thinking, or any daily changes you noticed in your heart or behavior.
3. *Look for contrasts.* Sometimes two readings or reflections might seem to stand in tension with each other. Often, such tensions highlight areas

for fruitful reflection. Write down the contrasting passages and any questions they raise. Meditate on them and pray about them—God may provide new illumination as you ponder!

4. *Form a small group.* You're not alone is seeking to deepen your spiritual life—so why not invite others to join you on your thirty-day journey with a great spiritual teacher? Try meeting weekly—whether over coffee or over a shared meal—to discuss that week's readings, reflections, and prayers. Talk to each other about how God is working in your lives. Pray together.

We hope that you'll be richly blessed by the books in this series. As you intentionally fill your days with the words and wisdom of a great spiritual teacher, we pray that you'll be ushered daily into the divine presence, experiencing more deeply than ever the life-giving joy of intimacy with the God who loves you.

The Publisher

THIRTY DAYS WITH
Frances Xavier Cabrini

DAY 1

My Day Begins

RETREAT NOTES, 1876, HOUSE OF PROVIDENCE, CODOGNO, ITALY

The end for which I was created is to serve and to love my God and Master, my sovereign creator with my whole being. He gave me such a small heart—and yet I want to divide it and reserve a little piece for my own selfish will, which my self-love thinks to be upright and holy. Ah, my Lord God, unfortunately I have been unstable like this all my life. At every hour and every moment, I have taken back a small piece of my heart which I have consecrated to you since my youth. What miserable ignorance! I have given my heart over to my whims, to my petty wishes, to my self-love which I still have.

Oh Lord, please help me! Come to my aid, enlighten me during these days so that I can make those resolutions that you know are necessary and always enlighten me so that I may truly put them into practice. Lord, I beg you to help me see that I am nothing, that "I" do not exist, that the "I" which I exalt is nothing but a ghost—a fictitious voice which will drag me to great ruin.

All Through the Day

Sacred Heart of Jesus, keep my heart focused solely on doing your will.

My Day Is Ending

O Sacred Heart of Jesus,
you've given me a heart to love you
and to serve you.
When I am tempted to save a part of my heart
for my own selfish will,
come to my aid
and save me from my selfish whims.
As I begin this thirty-day retreat,
I beg you to enlighten me

as you enlightened Mother Cabrini.
Help me to draw ever closer
to your Sacred Heart
so that my will may come fully into
communion with your will
and my actions and words
may bring hope to a weary world
just as Mother Cabrini's did.
Make me a missionary of hope for your people.

DAY 2

My Day Begins

RETREAT NOTES, 1877, HOUSE OF PROVIDENCE, CODOGNO, ITALY

I have felt a strong need for the Spiritual Exercises many times during this year. I feel that they would be useful for me at least twice a year so that your inspirations, wisdom, and mercy would always be with me. Instead, as the days pass, I waste time and energy, becoming depressed when I should be unwavering. In the light of the flames of your sweet heart, my dear Jesus, I see that I lack some of that lively and burning faith which should always flame ardently in my poor heart. . . .

Here, my Jesus, I am giving you a blank sheet of paper so you can write this beautiful virtue on my heart, followed by everything else that you want from me. Then I will sign it as a promise that I will never go back on my word. However, remember, my Jesus, that I am a poor weak thing, inert, ugly, full of many little evil habits that I never know how to let go of—in a word, full of what could frighten me. But I hope that this will not happen, knowing the truth that "I can do all things in you who strengthen me."

All Through the Day

Sacred Heart of Jesus, my heart is like a blank sheet of paper. Write the fire of your love on it.

My Day Is Ending

O Sacred Heart of Jesus,
may my faith always burn brightly in my heart.
I know that the best way to keep this flame going
is to spend time in conversation with you.
Making this thirty-day retreat is one little way
I can fan this flame.
With the help of your Holy Spirit,
may the fire of faith in my heart

grow bigger and bigger each day.
Just as Mother Cabrini knew that she needed
to make the Spiritual Exercises
of St. Ignatius regularly,
may I always feel the desire to make time
for prayers and retreats that help me turn
from evil habits and instead fill my heart
with hope and love.

DAY 3

My Day Begins

RETREAT NOTES, 1877, HOUSE OF PROVIDENCE, CODOGNO, ITALY

St. Ignatius showed me that it was the third degree of humility that I desire and truly want to practice with all my soul. Should it even cost my life, what does it matter? Life is fleeting. Therefore, I must be convinced in my mind that to practice the third degree of humility is to be open to take the royal way of suffering. Many times it will seem difficult, but what does it matter? . . . It is therefore necessary that I know that the greatest saints desired nothing more than to suffer and to continue suffering. Do I understand the importance of suffering? Then I am fortunate! Love live Jesus!

My Jesus, how I desire to be near you in the Garden of Olives where I see you abandoned in deep anguish! How much you suffer, my Jesus—and if I reflect on the reason for it, my God, what tremendous confusion! My sins are the cause for your bitter agony that even makes you sweat blood! Please, my Jesus, I beg you to forget my wickedness and allow me to watch beside you, allow me to say a word of comfort.

All Through the Day

Sacred Heart of Jesus, I offer up my sufferings
today to you.

My Day Is Ending

O Sacred Heart of Jesus,
help me to picture for a moment
the Garden of Olives,
with its ancient, gnarled trees
under which your disciples slept peacefully
while you, only a stone's throw away,
knelt in agonized prayer.
You suffered so deeply that you sweated blood.

I know that suffering is a part of this world
and that many saints understood
the importance of suffering.
They were willing to suffer insults, imprisonment,
poverty, and more
because they knew this was the way
to the deepest level of humility,
the way to imitating you.
Help me to offer up my sufferings
and to see them as a path to holiness and hope.

DAY 4

My Day Begins

RETREAT NOTES,
OCTOBER 22, 1878, HOUSE OF PROVIDENCE, CODOGNO, ITALY

"What profit would there be for one to gain the whole world and forfeit his life?" (Mt 16:26). These are the words which St. Ignatius of Loyola addressed to St. Francis Xavier, who then resolved firmly to give himself entirely and unreservedly to God. The same words will help us greatly to surrender generously to any desire of our Creator who loves us with such great mercy.

We do not come from ourselves and therefore, we are not created for ourselves, but to serve him alone in the way that he desires from us. It would make people laugh to see how we think so highly of ourselves sometimes—as if we were somebody important! We are being foolish when we complain something is not done the way we want it, without pondering whether it is purely for the glory of God or just something that we desire.

Even in things that are good, it is not advisable to be either overly troubled or overcome with melancholy when they do not turn out well, beautiful, and holy according to our way of thinking. From the moment that we were created, we deserve nothing and so we cannot expect anything. Therefore, in all things, whether holy, sweet, or bitter, we must always bless God with our whole hearts and repeat: "Lord, it is good when you permit things to happen that will help us to exercise the virtues that you are asking of us."

All Through the Day

Sacred Heart of Jesus, may everything I do be for the glory of God.

My Day Is Ending

O Sacred Heart of Jesus,
I want to give myself entirely
and unreservedly to you
just as St. Ignatius of Loyola, St. Francis Xavier,
and St. Frances Xavier Cabrini did.
While my heart may at times be
troubled or melancholic
when things don't go as I had hoped,
and I might wonder why you seem to deny me
even good and holy things,
my hope and my faith rest in you.
May I always bless you and thank you
for helping me to grow in virtue
through these unanswered prayers.
When I am tempted to think highly of myself,
remind me that it is only you
who can truly bring hope to the world.
I am merely your missionary.

DAY 5

My Day Begins

RETREAT NOTES, OCTOBER 21, 1882, CODOGNO, ITALY

But zeal is a great charity only when tempered with great love, as gentle as the love of the heart of Jesus. Gentle words move the hearts of even the most hardened sinners and lead them to repentance. I will strive always to be gentle in speaking. When words have no effect, I will resort to prayer and ask the heart of Jesus to touch their hearts. How much better he can accomplish this! Even during our daily ordinary tasks, whatever our work, let us offer every act to the heart of Jesus for the conversion of sinners. Even while sewing, let us make the intention that every stitch may pierce the heart of a sinner to arouse him to repentance.

May the exercises of the awareness of the presence of God be always alive within us. Let us see God in every object or person we encounter. Let us reflect on the omnipotence, wisdom, and bounty of our loving Jesus, just like those dear saints of the past who were so passionately in love with him.

All Through the Day

Sacred Heart of Jesus, I offer everything I do today for the conversion of sinners, including myself.

My Day Is Ending

O Sacred Heart of Jesus,
imbue me with the virtue of charity.
Help me to remember
to always be gentle in my speaking.
It is my hope that all people will come to know
your love and your wisdom.
When my gentle words fail
to bring others closer to you,

I will choose to pray for them instead.
I give to you every one of my actions,
even ordinary tasks like cleaning or cooking,
so that my prayer never ceases
and all of us will be called to repentance.

DAY 6

My Day Begins

RETREAT NOTES, DECEMBER 8, 1885, FEAST OF THE IMMACULATE CONCEPTION, CODOGNO, ITALY

How beautiful and radiant is Mary Immaculate! Loving Mother, enrich my poor soul with your splendid virtues. Heart of Jesus, I offer you the beauty of the Immaculate Heart of Mary to obtain mercy and full pardon of all my sins. How much I desire to please you who are loving Goodness itself. How sad I am to see myself so weak, so far from you. Look upon Mary's infinite merits, not on my faults, and draw me closer to your heart. . . .

My Immaculate Mother, I strongly desire to be humble and beg you to obtain this precious grace for me on your great feast. I am certain that you will give it to me so that I may truly please Jesus. Blessed

Margaret Alacoque, you who have inspired me to ask for this virtue so essential for true union with God, please ask Mary to obtain it from the heart of Jesus for me. God asks me to be faithful even in small things. And so, I will be vigilant and truly observant in order to please his loving heart.

All Through the Day

Sacred Heart of Jesus, may I imitate the example of your Blessed Mother and be faithful even in small things.

My Day Is Ending

O Sacred Heart of Jesus,
I want to please you in all of my actions.
I know I cannot do this on my own.
Therefore, I ask your Immaculate Mother,
who is my Immaculate Mother as well,
to beg on my behalf
so that my soul may be enriched

by the same virtues
of faith, hope, and trust that filled her heart.
Look not on my many faults,
but draw me ever closer to your loving heart
so that I may imitate your Mother
and point all people to you.

DAY 7

My Day Begins

RETREAT NOTES, FEBRUARY 15, 1888,
ROME, ITALY

My Jesus, I need to humble myself in your presence because I am so blind to my own faults and so expert in seeing the faults of my sisters. I am so sorry, Jesus. I know I am a poor, weak sinner, capable only of offending you. I humbly ask your pardon and promise to be continually on guard never to displease you. Yes, Jesus, I would prefer to accept my pain rather than offend you by the smallest sin.

Jesus, during these days, your love has penetrated me to such a depth that I do not know how to express my gratitude. You bind me to yourself and render me speechless, almost overpowered by so much goodness. My Jesus, beloved Spouse, I love you so much, so very much. I feel myself melting for love of you. Grant that my love is true and lasting and that the evil spirit will never deceive me.

All Through the Day

Sacred Heart of Jesus, I am overpowered
by your goodness.

My Day Is Ending

O Sacred Heart of Jesus,
why am I so good at seeing the faults of others
while being blind to my own?
When Mother Cabrini went on retreat,
she always humbled herself before you,
begging you to forgive her sins.
Each time, you rewarded her
with an overwhelming
amount of love, grace, and goodness.
I pray that during this thirty-day retreat
I may have a similar experience.
Help me to see where I have been blind

to my own faults, and, in return,
shower me with your goodness and grace.
I melt for love of you.

DAY 8

My Day Begins

LETTER TO HER MISSIONARY SISTERS, APRIL 19, 1890, SECOND VOYAGE TO NEW YORK

This morning we went on deck, saluted the sea, the image of the immensity of God, then we recited our prayers, which, without effort, came fervently from our souls. . . .

As soon as Sr. Battistina saw the boat move, she said she felt a dizziness in her head. Half an hour later she was very sick, and one after the other followed her example. I was the only one who remained unaffected. I wished the boat were steady, so that I might go on with my work, but I found I had to give up all idea of this. However, I continued to feel much better, and by degrees I felt I could breathe more freely. This, too, helped me to raise my soul to God, and I could almost say in all seriousness what I said jocularly a few days ago, that if the Sacred Heart would give me the means I would construct a boat called "The House of Cristoforo" ("Bearer of Christ") to traverse with one community, little or big, so as to carry the Name of Christ to all people, to those who as yet do not know him, and also to those who have forgotten Him.

All Through the Day

Sacred Heart of Jesus, help me to carry the name of Christ to all people.

My Day Is Ending

O Sacred Heart of Jesus,
some days my life feels like I'm on a rocky boat.
I want to do the work you've given me,
but one thing after another
seems to tip me from side to side.
Despite nearly drowning as a child
and her ensuing fear of the water,

Mother Cabrini crossed the seas sixty-seven times
because nothing was more important to her
than bringing the name of Christ to all people.
When things got rocky, she never failed to hope
that you would restore her peace and calm the sea.
Calm my rocky boat, Lord.
But if it pleases you that I endure
the rocky seas a little while longer,
then may I always rest in the hope
that you will answer my prayers
in your good timing.

DAY 9

My Day Begins

RETREAT NOTES, JULY 2, 1890,
MANRESA (WEST PARK), NEW YORK

"Speak, for your servant is listening" (1 Sam 3:10). Move my heart, enlighten my mind with a ray of your light and make me understand well what you want of me. I am ready for anything, even to give my life, so that I can achieve the perfection which you require from me. I do not trust myself because, unfortunately, I know my misery and weakness, but leaning on you, enclosed in your heart, I hope to do everything. "I have the strength for everything through him who empowers me" (Phil 4:13). . . .

Jesus, warm my heart with the fire of your holy love so that I will never fall into tepidity, but will always perform every action in your service with great fervor. In that way, I can make myself worthy to enter into you and abide in the sacred cavern of your most sweet heart, refuge of holy souls. Everything in nature speaks to me of you, beloved Jesus, and of the goodness of your heart. You called me to Manresa, you willed to donate this beautiful villa to me so that I could retire here in the days of my retreat. Please, speak to me, Lord, speak to me and I will listen to you, eager to follow your will faithfully.

All Through the Day

Sacred Heart of Jesus, speak so that I may know your will for me.

My Day Is Ending

O Sacred Heart of Jesus,
speak to me.
Whatever you ask me to do,
I know that I can succeed
because you will give me the strength to do it.
Everything in nature reminds me of you—
the sky, the land, the seas, the animals, and the birds.

Everything you give me is in service to you.
Just as you always seemed to find
the right location for Mother Cabrini's
next school, orphanage, or hospital,
may you always lead me
to the next right place to do your work.
Speak to me and tell me your will.
I am eager to follow you faithfully.

DAY 10

My Day Begins

LETTER TO HER MISSIONARY SISTERS, AUGUST 18, 1890, NEW YORK TO LE HAVRE

Oh, if everyone had knowledge of the great and beautiful advantages of meditation and of speaking familiarly with Jesus, if they could experience these heavenly joys, they would certainly envy our happy life (or state). Instead, how many poor creatures are there who do not want to know him, in order to follow their own passions more freely, blinded by the smoke of the false pleasures of the world! In these circumstances, and at the sight of so many miserable and unfortunate creatures, how much better we are able to understand the great grace that God has given us by calling us to his Divine Service, or, to express it more accurately, to his love. Let us love Jesus, then my daughters, let us love him very much. Jesus has ready for us many other graces, but he is waiting to be loved by us more and more, in order to grant these graces to us. On one occasion he said to one of his faithful servants that if he could find souls who would love him, as St. Francis of Assisi did, he would give us as many graces as he bestowed upon that saint, and even greater ones.

All Through the Day

Sacred Heart of Jesus, what a gift it is to speak familiarly with you!

My Day Is Ending

O Sacred Heart of Jesus,
I'm so grateful for this opportunity
to meditate on you
through the writings of St. Frances Xavier Cabrini.
They fill me with such hope!
After each meditation,
help me to continue in prayer
with you throughout my day.

What a joy it is to speak freely with you!
When I spend time in conversation with you,
you never fail to grant me special graces.
So many people in this world
do not know of your great love and mercy.
Help me to love you as Mother Cabrini did
so that, like her, I can bring you
many more souls to love.

DAY 11

My Day Begins

RETREAT NOTES, JULY 31, 1891, FEAST OF ST. IGNATIUS, CODOGNO, ITALY

May Mary, my Mother and teacher in the solitude of this retreat, gather me and all the other sisters under her mantle of special supervision and direction. Let me resemble her so that I may please Jesus, receive his divine grace, and acquire all her virtues. May my guardian angel be the guardian of my solitude and my instructor on every occasion. May St. Joseph, St. Francis Xavier, and St. Michael the Archangel intercede for me and make up for my great weakness which renders me unworthy of heavenly graces. "All for the greater honor and glory of the Sacred Heart of Jesus."

God, my Lord and Master, has created me, protected and helped me. What a great gift to be a servant of God, to be all his, irrevocably his! He thinks of me, and I surrender myself to his infinite goodness and mercy with boundless joy in my soul. He is my master, and I must serve him. What immense happiness! I can serve God and he accepts my poor service! Joyfully and enthusiastically, I surrender to him totally.

All Through the Day

Sacred Heart of Jesus, I surrender myself to you.

My Day Is Ending

O Sacred Heart of Jesus,
I want to do all things
for your greater honor and glory.
Help me to take my example
from your faithful servants,
such as your Blessed Mother, St. Joseph,
St. Ignatius of Loyola, St. Francis Xavier,
and St. Frances Xavier Cabrini.
They knew how to surrender themselves

totally to you
so that they could fulfill their role
in your project here on Earth.
Give me the protection of my guardian angel
and St. Michael the Archangel,
as I joyfully and enthusiastically
commit myself to your service.

DAY 12

My Day Begins

LETTER TO HER MISSIONARY SISTERS,
SEPTEMBER 10, 1891, LE HAVRE
TO NEW YORK

Last night the weather threatened to break and the sisters asked me if we were going to have good weather, because if it were bad they had made up their minds where to go and how to spend their time. I told them if we humbled ourselves profoundly for our faults, holding ourselves to blame for all the acts of frailty that seasickness caused us to commit, God would be propitious to us. At first some refused to acknowledge that they were in fault, saying it was the sea that caused so much discomfort, but remembering the promise they had made of suffering willingly for the holy cause of the Mission, they felt themselves obliged to humble themselves profoundly, and our dear Jesus in the truly paternal goodness of his heart granted us good weather, and so we are all assembled on the first class deck. You see, humility works wonders. All expected bad weather, and, instead, we have fine weather. Let us learn, dear daughters, to become humble, because God loves the humble, whilst he resists the proud. If we elevate ourselves through pride, God will withdraw from us, with the results that we fall into dense darkness. If we are humble, he will approach us, console us, and hear our prayer, and he will send us away justified. No, daughters, God does not make the humble wait long. He runs, flies to satisfy their holy and most excellent desires.

All Through the Day

Sacred Heart of Jesus, make me humble.

My Day Is Ending

O Sacred Heart of Jesus,
humility is a virtue our culture does not value.
However, you always seek out the humble.

You humbled yourself to become one of us.
Then you humbled yourself
to accept death on a cross.
Why? Because you love us!
And now you seek out those
who are humble like you.
Make me humble like you, Lord.
Help me to avoid pride so that
I do not fall into that dense darkness.
Instead, may I always be humble
and stay close to your Sacred Heart,
for it is only in humility
that I can bring your hope to the world.

DAY 13

My Day Begins

LETTER TO HER MISSIONARY SISTERS, OCTOBER 10, 1891, NEW YORK TO NICARAGUA

At 1 p.m. the anchor was raised and we glided slowly out of the port, while the sisters and friends waved their handkerchiefs. . . . Till evening we coasted along the shore, which we should have done all night, I believe, had not a terrific storm arisen which threatened to dash the boat and all it contained to pieces. At one moment the boat rolled from side to side with such force as to threaten to capsize. The sisters could hardly keep in their berths. I arose and dressed in haste to save them all, hoping at least to die together. Our luggage rolled about in all directions, like so many animated objects. There was nothing to stop it. No one could keep still, not even if seated on the floor. The sea swelled in an extraordinary way. The waves formed mountains as if by magic—one could see, as it were, deep valleys between them. The steamer seemed lost amidst these mountainous precipices of water. The wind worked havoc on deck, and threatened to split the cabins, but limited its caprice to the doctor's only. . . .

But, God be praised! For during the terrible storm, as the Captain told us, no one was lost or hurt. . . . I was praying to Our Lady of the Holy Rosary, in whose month we were voyaging. Then I lighted the candle of Our Lady of Loretto, so efficacious against sea storms, and our Most Holy Mother did really come to our aid, delivering us from the extreme danger which surrounded us!

All Through the Day

Sacred Heart of Jesus, in times of trouble,
may I always turn to you in prayer.

My Day Is Ending

O Sacred Heart of Jesus,
when faced with a challenging situation,

it can be easy to think we must run around,
taking control of everyone
and everything, even nature.
While it is good to care for one another
and look out for one another,
sometimes the best we can do is pray and hope.
When I am faced with a situation
where I've done all I can do,
I will turn to the Rosary and pray
for peace in my heart,
trusting that our Holy Mother
will carry our intentions to you
so that you can protect us and guide us.

DAY 14

My Day Begins

LETTER TO HER MISSIONARY SISTERS, OCTOBER 15, 1891, NEW YORK TO NICARAGUA

Today is the 15th of October, the Feast of St. Teresa [of Avila], and this saint, who had sufferings of all kinds and had long and painful experiences, has obtained for us a most beautiful day: a clear sky, a vast horizon, and a pure gentle breeze. One could imagine that we were at Heaven's gates, from whence emanates a sweet comfort to enable us, as it were, to partake of the grand and beautiful feast which Jesus gives his Beloved Spouse. There is no priest on board, so no Mass, but we have been able to communicate spiritually with great faith. That fortunate prisoner had reason to rejoice at the thought that she once held Jesus in her heart, and entering, as it were into the Mystical Tabernacle of her Soul, rejoiced as if she really held her Beloved. We, happier still, have received him many times, and it is only five days ago that our hearts beat together with his, and that he worked with us and was given to us in Holy Viaticum. Today, then, it was not difficult to draw ourselves around Jesus in order that he might charm our hearts, as he once pierced the heart of the Seraph of Carmel.

All Through the Day

Sacred Heart of Jesus, pierce my heart
with your love.

My Day Is Ending

O Sacred Heart of Jesus,
do I truly appreciate the gift of you
in the Eucharist?
It can be so easy to take you for granted
when I receive you in Holy Communion.
For many of us, we are surrounded
by multiple opportunities each day

to attend Mass and receive you.
Mother Cabrini and her sisters
often traveled for weeks
without being able to attend Mass.
In parts of the world, there are not enough priests
for everyone to receive Communion weekly,
much less daily.
When I do receive you,
help me to be grateful for the gift of you.
And when I cannot receive you,
help me to hold you in my heart.

DAY 15

My Day Begins

RETREAT NOTES, NOVEMBER 9, 1893,
GENOA, ITALY

Jesus has inspired me to ask for total surrender and perfect self-detachment as the fruit of this retreat, so that I can be filled with his grace. In the important affairs I have at hand for this foundation, I will not be upset by the trials and contradictions I encounter. I will always show a cheerful countenance, certain that what happens will be no more or no less than what God wants, whatever is pleasing to him.

Jesus has told me clearly during these days: "You think of me and I will think of your affairs." My Jesus, how good and loving you are. You think more of me and my affairs than I myself do. I surrender myself totally to all your plans and, from now on, I will say joyfully and enthusiastically in my soul: "Your kingdom come, your will be done" (Mt 6:10). . . .

My Jesus, your voice is so powerful! Following it brings such peace, sweetness, and joy that my soul is overwhelmed. Oh sacred sea of Love, I immerse myself totally in you. Oh sea of immense joy, guide me however you want, as the great pilot of my little boat. Bring me wherever you want so that I may in some way serve and console your divine heart.

In order to be imprinted with the likeness of Jesus and be conformed to his holy life, it is necessary to prepare our souls, just like the photographer who prepares whatever is necessary to produce a dear image of his subject. We too must prepare and exercise all our powers in meditating with lively faith, profound humility, holy desires, and burning love.

All Through the Day

Sacred Heart of Jesus, be the great pilot who steers my life.

My Day Is Ending

O Sacred Heart of Jesus,
so many times I want to wrest control
of my life out of your hands
and control everything according to my plan.
Help me to practice detachment
as St. Ignatius encouraged.
Whether things go the way I plan
or whether they go differently than I'd hoped,
help me to accept the outcome cheerfully,
knowing that following your divine plan
will bring me peace, joy, and hope.
St. Thérèse reminded us
that this world is our ship and not our home.
St. Frances reminds us
that you are the pilot of this ship.
Steer us home to you, Lord.

DAY 16

My Day Begins

LETTER TO HER MISSIONARY SISTERS, SEPTEMBER 21, 1894, GENOA TO NEW YORK

Yesterday the staff were making great preparations to protect us from the icebergs of Newfoundland, as we shall be very close to them tonight, but the precautions were not needed, for the Blessed Virgin covered us with her mantle, the Holy Souls interceded for us, and the result was that we had rain during the whole night, which proved very advantageous, for the sea became quite calm. Fresh water and salty water mixed together form a calm sea, and this lesson teaches us how to behave with those who are against us. Raise your hearts on high and accept God's will without murmuring against or criticizing those people who afflict us. Pity them and excuse them as did David with regard to his enemy, for, on hearing himself reviled he did not defend himself, but said, "Let them talk, because it is God who permits their speaking against me, it is little indeed, they are saying, I merit more." Thus behaves a soul according to the heart of God. If we become possessors of such virtues, we would become saints very easily. Never murmur, never criticize; if you are inclined to use your tongue, use it against yourself. Or, better still, as St. Francis de Sales inculcates, say neither good nor bad of yourself.

All Through the Day

Sacred Heart of Jesus, infuse the words I will speak today with hope, love, and encouragement.

My Day Is Ending

O Sacred Heart of Jesus,
just as fresh water and salt water mix together
to form a calm sea,
help me to accept both criticism and praise
with humility and calmness.

Let me be like King David,
who did not defend himself
from those who spoke out against him,
knowing it was possible
that he merited even more criticism.
Let me be like St. Frances Xavier Cabrini,
who neither murmured against nor criticized
those who afflicted her.
Let me be like St. Francis de Sales,
who encouraged people not to use their tongues
to brag or belittle themselves.
May the words I speak always be
words of hope, love, and encouragement.

DAY 17

My Day Begins

RETREAT NOTES, CHRISTMAS 1894
TO JANUARY 1, 1895, NEW YORK

When Jesus entered triumphantly into Jerusalem, many good people had prepared a banquet, desiring to invite him into their homes. Later, because of human respect and fear of the scribes who threatened those who honored Jesus, they left him alone and fasting. Poor Jesus, I am not worthy, but I would like you to come to my house for dinner. Put your hand on my head and enrich me with your grace so I may entertain you well. At table, let me occupy a seat at the place of trust at your left side, so I can serve you well and have you served in everything. Then, let me rest my head on your heart that I may understand all your divine secrets and understand clearly all that you desire of me. I want to do all things well for you. Grant that I never keep you waiting at the door of my heart.

All Through the Day

Sacred Heart of Jesus, knock at the door of my heart, and I will let you in.

My Day Is Ending

O Sacred Heart of Jesus,
what a privilege Lazarus, Martha, and Mary had
when they welcomed you
into their home for dinner.
I want to welcome you into my home too.
But more than that,
I hope to welcome you fully into my heart.
Once I have allowed you
to fully make your home in me,
I know I will learn to treat all guests
as if I were entertaining and serving you.
Fill my heart with hope

as I strive to do all things
for the greater honor and glory
of your Sacred Heart.

DAY 18

My Day Begins

LETTER TO HER MISSIONARY SISTERS, JUNE 1, 1895, NEW ORLEANS TO PANAMA

By the words of consecration said by the priest in the name of Jesus, the bread is changed or transubstantiated into the body of Jesus, and so the body and blood are present under the appearances of bread and of wine by a miracle of the Omnipotent. After the Consecration, the substance of the bread and wine disappear, the appearances only remaining, like so many veils of love and wisdom to hide from our material eyes our glorious Lord's presence, as also to supply motives for faith, confidence, and courage in receiving our Divine Lord into our hearts. As long as the species remains, so long does the Sacramental Presence last, as soon as the species is consumed, the most Sacred Body retires and vanishes. Nothing but wonders are worked on the Altar. The priests, who, during the twenty-four hours, offer the Divine Sacrifice in so many countries, towns, and villages all the world over, are innumerable, and thus in a hundred thousand places Jesus is present in the sacrament of his love. Could there be an invention more beautiful and more holy than the institution of this most divine sacrament? Could the Loving Jesus show us a greater tenderness of love?

All Through the Day

Sacred Heart of Jesus, thank you for showing us
the tenderness of your love.

My Day Is Ending

O Sacred Heart of Jesus,
I may never fully understand
the miracle that occurs
each time the bread and wine
are transubstantiated

into your very body and blood.
Despite my lack of understanding,
my hope and my faith rest in you.
All day long, all around the world,
you come to your people
through the Divine Sacrifice of the Holy Mass.
May we all come to a greater appreciation
of your tender love for us through
the Holy Eucharist.

DAY 19

My Day Begins

LETTER TO HER MISSIONARY SISTERS, OCTOBER 17, 1895, PANAMA DOWN THE PACIFIC AND ACROSS THE ANDES TO BUENOS AIRES

Yesterday we left Ecuador and entered the waters of Peru, and at seven a.m. we arrived at the port of Paita. It looks like a city of desolation, and at first sight it saddens one's heart. No trees, no grass, no fountain are visible. Surrounded by low and dry mountains, it is a real desert. Yet it is one of the most healthy ports, and large numbers even from Ecuador come here to enjoy its curative advantages. In fact, the air one breathes here is pure, light, and balsamic, and really restores one. The sea is tranquil, and they tell us it never gets rough at this point. It has such a beautiful blue soft color that one would think it a fallen portion of the sky. But to us it appeared even more beautiful and singular, for, as we looked around to see if we could find a steeple to which we could turn our thoughts to Jesus in the Blessed Sacrament of the Altar, a flock of white birds suddenly whirled around us, making a strange noise, at which Mother Chiara broke silence, saying, "What can this mean?"

"Oh," I replied, playfully, "they are inviting us to their country as they did three years ago at Panama, and we will go there when we can."

All Through the Day

Sacred Heart of Jesus, may I see you in every aspect of nature.

My Day Is Ending

O Sacred Heart of Jesus,
do I see you in the sky or the sea or the birds?
When I look at trees and grass
or mountains and snow,
do I consider how they all came from you?

Mother Cabrini always turned her thoughts to you.
When her boat entered new ports
or even passed by new towns,
she sought out church steeples
to find your presence
waiting within the tabernacle below.
At the same time, she could see you
in the natural beauty
she encountered in each new land she visited
and could even find an invitation from you
through the very birds in the air.
May I always keep my eyes open
in the hope that I may see you in all things.

DAY 20

My Day Begins

RETREAT NOTES, SEPTEMBER 1897, CODOGNO, ITALY

Jesus, what can disturb the peace and joy you put in my heart? Tribulations, adversities, contradictions? No, my Jesus, at the sound of your voice, I rest in you and my peace increases, instead of diminishing. True heavenly peace consists in the perfect accomplishment of your will, without seeking or desiring anything else. "Let me hear your voice" (Sg 2:14). Jesus, let me hear the sound of your voice which enchants my soul. I will follow you tirelessly, wholeheartedly, because the sound of your voice works miracles in my soul, moving it gently toward you. Jesus, Jesus, how dear and loving you are! I love you so much, so very much! The humble and spiritually indifferent soul is not disturbed by adversity, humiliations, insults, or being forgotten. Rather, she rejoices that she is growing closer to her greatest Good and so will enjoy unshakable peace of soul.

Jesus, let your voice sound that I may understand what you want of me, that I may always find you to love you, know you to imitate you, love you to possess you, possess you to enjoy you. You want me to seek you with all my affections, to find, know, love, and glorify you. I will strive with all the strength you give me to make you served and honored by all.

All Through the Day

Sacred Heart of Jesus, my hope in you is so strong that my peace is unshakeable.

My Day Is Ending

O Sacred Heart of Jesus,
if I put my trust in you, I will never lose hope.
No tribulations, no adversities
can take away my peace.
When I hear your voice and know your will,

I need only listen and obey.
This is the kind of unshakeable peace
that comes only from loving you.
And if I truly love you,
then I will imitate you.
And by imitating you,
I will honor and glorify you.

DAY 21

My Day Begins

LETTER TO HER MISSIONARY SISTERS, NOVEMBER 5, 1898, LIVERPOOL TO NEW YORK

I was comforted by the blessing of the Holy Father, who at the end of July gave me an audience and encouraged me, with benignity, to go all over the world and carry the Most Holy Name of Jesus everywhere, thus to draw souls into the bosom of the Church, where alone there is salvation. With fatherly goodness he inquired about my program, and noticing my poor health, he asked how I could undertake so much work. "I, who am so strong, could not do it," he said. "It is true that I am old, but I am much stronger than you." The affability with which he deigned to speak to me, encouraged me to remark that, as I was his spiritual daughter, I possessed his moral strength which enabled me to go around the world, and I was sure I should not lose my strength by serving that dear Jesus Who chose me to be a Missionary of his Sacred Heart. . . .

Do pray, daughters, pray for the Holy Father, pray for the Ruler of Church's destiny, pray for him in these difficult times. We must do so, as we are under obligations of filial gratitude to Leo XIII, who loves and favors our beloved Institute as if it were his own beloved family.

All Through the Day

Sacred Heart of Jesus, I offer up today's work
for the intentions of the Holy Father.

My Day Is Ending

O Sacred Heart of Jesus,
it can be hard to practice obedience to your will.
St. Frances wanted to be a missionary to China.
However, Pope Leo XIII asked her
to go to the West and not the East.
Because she vowed to be obedient,

she followed his instructions faithfully.
This obedience proved so fruitful
that he then encouraged her
to carry your holy name around the world.
In turn, she encouraged her sisters
to pray for the Holy Father.
Lord, I pray today for our pope.
May he be a true shepherd to your people
so that we can continue to carry
your Holy Name everywhere.

DAY 22

My Day Begins

RETREAT NOTES, JUNE 1899, MANRESA (WEST PARK), NEW YORK

The victim soul who is grateful to God never complains! She never says "enough"—accepting physical and spiritual pains, labors and community duties, contradictions and difficulties—all are small. She receives everything with great generosity and unlimited confidence in God. Being humble, she is not afraid of death or the loss of herself and goes ahead, following Jesus until the consummation of her sacrifice.

The essence of sanctity consists in recognizing the sovereignty of God over us and being submissive to him, surrendering in silence and in peace without complaining about the lack of human comforts. This is the goal which the soul consecrated to God must achieve. Let us regard afflictions as a guardian angel, a beneficent shadow that prevents the burning sun of earthly things from drying up our prayer and virtue. . . .

It is not important to accomplish great and visible works—the most important thing is to do well *what* Jesus wants of us, in the *manner* he wants it done, and in the *circumstances* he desires.

All Through the Day

Sacred Heart of Jesus, help me to do what you want, when you want it, and in the manner you desire.

My Day Is Ending

O Sacred Heart of Jesus,
it is so easy to complain when I am in pain,
whether that pain is physical,
spiritual, or emotional.
Your great saints like St. Frances Xavier Cabrini
teach me that I should receive these pains
with hope and gratitude

as part of my complete surrender to your will.
Like my guardian angel,
these afflictions in my life
keep my prayer time from drying up.
They keep me focused on you
and what you want of me.
May I focus not so much on doing great things
but on having a fruitful prayer life
that helps me do your will exactly
how, when, and where you want me to do so.

DAY 23

My Day Begins

LETTER TO HER MISSIONARY SISTERS, SEPTEMBER 5, 1899, NEW YORK TO LE HAVRE

We all went to table, but, after the first course, everybody, one after another, left, as the steamer swayed from one side to the other. We were naturally upset. Mother Virginia fled to her bed; it is the only place for her when the steamer rocks. At our table, only the Marist Sister and I remained until dinner was over, and then we took a walk on deck, thanking God for having made us such good sailors. But the rocking increased and the air turned colder, so I thought I would go to bed also. About nine-thirty the silence was broken by the foghorn. This is a sign of great fog, and is blown to call the attention of others steamers which may be coming in the same direction, as it is impossible to see them amidst such dense darkness. The movement still continued, but, fortunately, it was of a rolling character rather than a pitching one, but the quite unusual activity of the crew frightened us as well as the other passengers. Coincidentally, the points of our meditation spoke of the storm which tossed the apostles, and so we became quiet at the thought of the beautiful words of Jesus to his beloved apostles, "*Habete fiduciam*," and "*Ego sum. Nolite timere.*" In fact, having our beloved Jesus with us, why need we fear? He is the master of creation, and all creatures obey him.

All Through the Day

Sacred Heart of Jesus, with you by my side, I will have no fear.

My Day Is Ending

O Sacred Heart of Jesus,
what a picture of hope and trust is Mother Cabrini!
Despite nearly drowning as a child

and developing a fear of water,
she crossed the sea repeatedly
to bring your name to all people.
No storm on the sea could shake
her confidence in you.
She need only remember what you
told your apostles:
"Have courage. It is I. Do not be afraid."
After all, you are the Master of Creation.
All creation must obey you.
When I am afraid, help me
to place all hope in you.
You are the answer to all my fears.

DAY 24

My Day Begins

LETTER TO HER MISSIONARY SISTERS, DECEMBER 3, 1900, FEAST OF ST. FRANCIS XAVIER, GENOA TO BUENOS AIRES

Let us imagine we are like St. Francis Xavier, and always keep our Divine Lord before us, beholding his mild gravity, his quiet amiability, his unalterable evenness of temper. In thus copying his Divine Model, we shall see how he worked, walked, spoke, and taught. . . .

This beautiful feast day we mostly passed in the port of Barcelona. We thought we were going to hear several Masses, as on December 2, but we ran the risk of not having even one, as nearly all the priests went on shore. However, the admirable Providence of God, Who watches over us, wished to console us by way of a special favor. The only priest who had arranged to celebrate on board, arose quite early to say Mass, as he intended going to visit the city after. But he could not find the key of the case in which he kept his sacred vestments. It happened that we had just got up, and met the priest at his wits' end because of the lost key. He was, indeed, about to take breakfast. "No, Father," I said, "look again and you will find it, because we want to hear Mass to celebrate the feast of our holy patron." So he went to make another search for it, and he found it where he least expected it, to his great joy. . . . We regarded this as a pleasant surprise from our holy patron, who, from the beginning of our missions, has never ceased to show his admirable generosity towards us.

All Through the Day

Sacred Heart of Jesus, thank you for always watching over me.

My Day Is Ending

O Sacred Heart of Jesus,
do I recognize all the ways
you intervene on my behalf,

or when things seem to turn out right
at the last minute,
am I tempted to chalk it all up to coincidence?
Do I look to your saints and ask
for their intervention,
trusting beyond all hope
that they will have your ear?
Mother Cabrini and her sisters knew
that if the priest had found his key sooner,
they would've missed Mass that day.
Their patron, St. Francis Xavier,
knew of their desire
to receive you in the Eucharist on his feast day,
and so he intervened for them.
When special favors are granted to me,
help me to see your loving hand at work.

DAY 25

My Day Begins

RETREAT NOTES, SEPTEMBER 1902,
ST. MICHAEL'S FEAST, CODOGNO, ITALY

After a long month of travel, how consoling it is for me to make the Spiritual Exercises, to look into my soul and compare it with the heart of my Jesus, to see if all my attitudes are similar to his and can give him pleasure. May my guides be: Mary, my caring mother; St. Joseph, my teacher; and St. Michael, the special angel of the Institute. May I learn from this experience for the greater glory of the Sacred Heart of Jesus and the sanctification of my soul. . . .

Jesus, if my beloved brothers and sisters would have had all the gifts and graces that you have so generously and mercifully bestowed upon me through the goodness of your divine heart, they would already have become great saints. Instead I find myself still miserable and poor, lacking every virtue and possessing only basic good will, which I also recognize as a gift of your immense goodness. I greatly desire holiness in order to please you, but my poverty impedes me from reaching the goal I long to achieve.

Beloved Jesus, my health is uncertain and paradise is not secure, but this uncertainty is good for me and floods my soul with a new joy. I find myself in the happy condition of loving and serving you as a beloved daughter and not as a servant. My good Jesus, give me the grace to love you with all my heart and to serve you with great fidelity in this life, so that I can be a grain of sand to build up your glory for all eternity.

All Through the Day

Sacred Heart of Jesus, make all my attitudes
similar to yours today.

My Day Is Ending

O Sacred Heart of Jesus,
do I recognize the role I play

in building up your glory for all eternity,
even if it means my contribution
is no bigger than a grain of sand?
Mother Cabrini found great happiness in realizing
that she served you as a beloved daughter
and not as a servant.
Fill my heart with this same joy.
Make me grateful and hopeful,
trusting in you, my beloved Jesus,
to give me the gifts and the graces I need
to bring greater glory to your Sacred Heart.

DAY 26

My Day Begins

LETTER TO HER MISSIONARY SISTERS, ON THE OCCASION OF THE INAUGURATION OF THE HOUSE IN DENVER, NOVEMBER 18, 1902, DENVER, COLORADO

The world is poisoned with erroneous theories, and needs to be taught sane doctrines, but it is difficult to straighten what has become crooked. It is in your hands to form new generations, to lead them in the right direction, to instill into them those principles which are the seed of good works, though for the moment they may seem hidden. The impressions of childhood are never obliterated. We shall be indebted to you, if the youth whom you educate, when grown up, become the pride of the family, of society, of the state, and, especially, the honor and support of our holy faith. . . .

Work, then, while you have time. Work with energy, and especially with the spirit of sacrifice, for it is this that forms the true missionary. This storms the heart of Jesus, and draws from it, as it were, the most precious graces for those souls who are the hardest and the most obstinate in resisting his love. Work with an apostolic spirit which offers everything, actions, prayers and sacrifices for the conversion of souls.

All Through the Day

Sacred Heart of Jesus, help me to plant good seeds in the next generation.

My Day Is Ending

O Sacred Heart of Jesus,
children will never forget the impressions
we leave on them.
Whether we are parents or teachers,
aunts or uncles,
or simply neighbors and friends,

the children in our lives are watching us.
They are learning how to become
people of goodwill and good works.
Help us to form the next generation,
especially those young people
who are most resistant
to receiving your great love.
May we be inspired by Mother Cabrini's words
to work with energy and a spirit of sacrifice
to give others a sense of hope
for as long as you give us time to do your work.

DAY 27

My Day Begins

RETREAT NOTES, DECEMBER 8, 1903, FEAST OF THE IMMACULATE CONCEPTION, SEATTLE, WASHINGTON

Jesus, you are a sublime mystery of love for me. I desire to know you in order to love you, to love you in order to serve you. I love you, my Jesus, I love you so much, so very much, but I am not satisfied—I want to love you even more. I want to be consumed with love for you. . . .

Even if I would be totally consumed, I would not be doing much for you, my God. Of myself, I am nothing and good for nothing. But God, do with me what you want—place me wherever you like. With your grace, I will live fully surrendered, trusting in your loving heart.

There I will seek to remain enclosed, repeating: "I have the strength for everything through him who empowers me" (Phil 4:13). Yes, I am nothing and of no value, but with the help of my beloved spouse, I can do all things. I can do great things for your glory, if you want it. I only have to be faithful, not attributing anything to my own efforts. If I thought myself to be someone important or capable, everyone would have the right to come after me as if I were a raving lunatic! My Jesus, I always want to live with childlike simplicity of heart, seeking you always in simplicity. Simplicity and surrender to you will be the strong wings with which I can always fly to you, soaring over earth's miseries, far away from the enemies of holiness.

All Through the Day

Sacred Heart of Jesus, grant me childlike
simplicity to trust in you.

My Day Is Ending

O Sacred Heart of Jesus,
Mother Cabrini's undying hope lay

in her complete trust in you.
She knew she could do nothing on her own.
However, with you all things were possible.
You gave her wings to travel across vast oceans,
negotiate shrewd business deals,
and find funding for schools,
orphanages, and hospitals,
even when there seemed to be no money available.
She convinced hundreds of women
to follow her lead.
When I am tempted to think I can do nothing,
remind me to stop putting my trust in myself.
Rather, let me place all my hope in you,
so that, like Mother Cabrini, you will
give me wings
to soar over Earth's miseries.

DAY 28

My Day Begins

LETTER TO THE STUDENTS OF THE TEACHERS' COLLEGE IN ROME, MAY 1904

How great, noble, exalted, is the mission you are called to accomplish in this world! To you, Our Divine Lord addressed the words he spoke to his apostles one day, "I have chosen you so that you will bear fruit and that your fruit will remain." Reflect a little with me on the predilection of God for you in this call. "I have chosen you," not "You have chosen Me." In fact, he did not wish that during your studies you should be exposed to the poisonous atmosphere of the world. . . . However small your experience is of the world, still you see that the multitude is insensible, forgetting God. But how much good cannot a wise teacher do to repair this, the greatest of evils, if to her mental culture and her intellectual gifts she adds that of a soul solidly founded and frankly Christian and religious. . . . She knows that those who have not received in their early years the impressions of religion, grow up without having even the slightest idea of those high truths which alone can awaken in them the love of virtue and the control of the passions. She then makes her sweet influence felt in the school, aided by the grace of the Holy Ghost, and silently molds those young hearts which, soft as wax, are ready to receive impressions.

All Through the Day

Sacred Heart of Jesus, thank you for choosing me
to bring your empire of hope to others.

My Day Is Ending

O Sacred Heart of Jesus,
Mother Cabrini reminded those
studying to become teachers
that God had chosen them,
but truly you have chosen each of us

to use our own "sweet influence" to bear fruit.
With the help of the Holy Spirit,
help me to bring your hope
to all those who have never known you
or have forgotten you.
Make me ever ready for this noble mission
you have entrusted to me,
so that I can, in my own small way,
participate in bringing about your empire of hope.

DAY 29

My Day Begins

LETTER TO THE STUDENTS OF THE TEACHERS' COLLEGE IN ROME, MAY 1905

We had, in the foundation of the Chicago Hospital, a visible proof showing how powerfully Heaven helps those who invoke with faith. . . . When I arrived in Chicago to complete all arrangements in the hospital which was to be opened on February 26, I found there were two months more work to be done. The date of opening had, however, been fixed, and it could not be changed. . . .

The sisters worked day and night. The work seemed to increase instead of decreasing. People even remarked, "It is too much; it cannot be finished—there are too many difficulties ahead." But firm trust in the heart of Jesus kept us calm, and amidst this tranquility the work was quickly and well done, so much so that on February 28 we were able to open the doors of the hospital, and at the same time feel sure the critical eye of the public would have no reason to find fault or ridicule.

It was a great day for the New Columbus Hospital. We called it "The Day of the Lord," as it was all his work. Even a most clear sky, with a sun which made the blue waters of the immense Lake Michigan sparkle, seemed to participate in the feast.

All Through the Day

Sacred Heart of Jesus, with you all
things are possible.

My Day Is Ending

O Sacred Heart of Jesus,
you never failed to come to Mother Cabrini's aid.
When others told her a job was impossible,
she did not hesitate to press forward,
even when resources were lacking
and time was short.

She knew that you would make all things possible.
When I am facing a seemingly impossible task,
help me to work with the same sense of tranquility
that kept Mother Cabrini calm,
so that I can press onward
with a heart filled with hope
because I know that I can do all things
through you who strengthen me.

DAY 30

My Day Begins

LETTER TO THE STUDENTS OF THE TEACHERS' COLLEGE IN ROME, FEBRUARY 1906

There is room for everybody, for every activity, for every talent and for every inclination. She who consecrates herself to Jesus as a Missionary Sister, willing to carry his name even to the utmost ends of the earth, sacrificing her dearest affection and even life itself, is a true heroine in whose heart the flame of love burns brightly. She does not stifle her own heart nor put under a bushel the shining light of intelligence with which God has endowed her. On the contrary, the flame kindled in her heart becomes a regular volcano of love which embraces everything. That gleam of light becomes a brilliant torch, causing darkness to disappear and erring souls to find their way. Happy the one who, at the tribunal of

God, will be able to present herself followed by a great number of souls saved through her.

All Through the Day

Sacred Heart of Jesus, may I one day present you with a great number of souls whom I have played a small role in leading to you.

My Day Is Ending

O Sacred Heart of Jesus,
as this thirty-day retreat comes to an end,
I look forward to carrying the lessons
I've learned from Mother Cabrini into the world.
I will not hide my heart, burning with love for you.
I will not shy away from carrying the flame
you have kindled in my heart to everyone I meet.
May my words and my actions
help to disperse the darkness
so that your empire of hope
will reign in every heart.

Notes

1. Mary Louise Sullivan, *Mother Cabrini: "Italian Immigrant of the Century"* (Center for Migration Studies, 1992), 40.

2. Theodore Maynard, *Too Small a World: The Life of Mother Frances Cabrini* (Ignatius Press, 2024), 108.

3. Frances Xavier Cabrini, *Journal of a Trusting Heart: Retreat Notes of St. Frances Xavier Cabrini, 1876–1911* (Claretian Publications, 2023), 86.

Frances Cabrini (1850–1917) was a pioneering Catholic missionary who dedicated her life to serving the underserved. She founded the Missionary Sisters of the Sacred Heart of Jesus, an order focused on education, health care, and social services. In 1889, Pope Leo XIII sent her to New York City to minister to the growing population of Italian immigrants, and she quickly became a champion for their needs. Over the course of her life, she established sixty-seven institutions worldwide, including schools, hospitals, and orphanages, all grounded in her unwavering faith and commitment to human dignity. In recognition of her exceptional holiness, compassion, and tireless service, she was canonized a saint by Pope Pius XII in 1946. Four years later, she was named the Patroness of Immigrants, further cementing her legacy as a symbol of hope and solidarity for those in need.

Amy J. Cattapan is a middle-school English teacher, Catholic speaker, retreat leader, and author who has written or contributed to several books, including *Sweet Jesus, Is It June Yet?*, *A Saint Squad for Teachers*, *Chicken Soup for the Soul: From Lemons to Lemonade*, and (as A.J. Cattapan) the award-winning novels *Angelhood* and *Seven Riddles to Nowhere*. She hosts *Cath-Lit Live!*, a podcast where she interviews Catholic authors about new books.

Cattapan has appeared on *The Katie McGrady Show* and *The Busted Halo Show* on SiriusXM, EWTN's *Bookmark* and *At Home with Jim and Joy*, *Catholic Faith Network Live*, and the *Son Rise Morning Show*. Her writing has appeared in *Highlights for Children*, *Hopscotch for Girls*, *Pockets*, and *Catechist*. She also served as the host for Shalom World TV's BOOK.ed.

Cattapan earned a bachelor's degree in English secondary education from Marquette University, a master's degree in instruction for secondary education language arts from Northeastern Illinois University, and a doctorate in curriculum and instruction from Loyola University Chicago. She has spoken at a variety of conferences, including the National Catholic Educational Association, the Los Angeles Religious Education Congress, and C3, and frequently leads teacher retreats and professional development sessions at Catholic schools across the country.

Cattapan lives in Buffalo Grove, Illinois.

www.ajcattapan.com
Facebook: acattapan
X: @AJcattapan
Instagram: @a.j.cattapan
Pinterest: @ajcattapan
YouTube: A.J. Cattapan